DEDICATION

*To my friend, Rick Jeffers, and his dedication to living his life
based on his values. While his life was cut short, he lived it to the fullest.
If a genuine smile and the ability to make others feel better about
themselves were not on his list of personal core values,
I would be surprised! Rick and his example of living his core values
will be tremendously missed.*

*Also dedicated to those brave souls who strive to live their core values
in every breath of their life ... regardless of the cost.*

Published by Simple Truths, LLC
1952 McDowell Road, Suite 205
Naperville, IL 60563

Design: Rich Nickel
Edited by: Stephanie Trannel
Illustrations by: Wilkinson Studios, Inc.
iStock Photos: 5, 18, 24, 28, 35, 57, 67
Getty Photos: 73, 83, 93, 107

Printed and bound in the United States of America

ISBN 978-1-60810-022-4

simple truths®
THE GIFT OF INSPIRATION

www.simpletruths.com
(800) 900-3427

01 WOZ 09

GOOD to the CORE

Building Value With Values

JOHN G. BLUMBERG

Contents

Section One — INVESTIGATE the Value of Values

Section Two — INDICATE Your Own Core Values

Section Three   **INTEGRATE Your Values and Actions**

Introduction

It wasn't a life and death situation. It wasn't going to cost him millions of dollars. And his job wasn't on the line. But as a soccer coach with a 0-0 tie, a game against one of the top-ranked teams in the state was on the line. The referee made a call that set up the perfect free kick that could put his team in the lead with only 10 minutes to go. But he knew the ref had made a really bad call … in his favor. Instead of having his star forward slam the ball at the vulnerable goalie, he instructed her to rather softly roll the ball to the goalie so she could simply pick it up and put it back into play. Victory was certainly important to him. Just not as important as his values.

*I have yet to meet anyone who would say
they didn't want to operate from a position of a solid set
of values. I think most of us want to be good to the core.
On the surface, the concept of values is intellectually
easy to understand. And so I assumed,
and maybe you do too, that most of us understand
and try to live by our values.*

An assumption can be a dangerous thing. Especially when it comes to the core. And trying to live something that at best is vague, or at worst doesn't actually exist, is virtually impossible!

I had always assumed you could give most professional adults a blank sheet of paper and ask them to write down their core values, and with minimal effort they could list them. I couldn't have been more wrong. Very few can.

My assumption that outstanding college students know their personal core values delivers similar dismal results. When you ask most professionals to write down their organization's values … the likelihood of them listing the values correctly gets even slimmer.

I am not the only one making an assumption. In fact, many of us just assume we know our values. Some will say, "I have a gut feeling about my values." Or they might say, "I generally understand my company's values." I would say a "gut feeling" or a "general understanding" is a dangerous formula in a world that is moving exponentially faster each day. It is dangerous for both you and for the organization where you work.

When it comes to corporations, associations, universities or any other organization, the bottom-line is that values are valuable to their "bottom-line." It impacts mission, vision, retention, service, and ultimately the very culture of the organization. **Even so, many organizations are winging it!**

There are many examples of organizations with stated values. A subset of that group may even put great emphasis on employees knowing those values. A subset of that group might have gone so far as to create a culture that encourages (or even demands) everyone live and hold others accountable to the stated values. And a subset of that group truly measures and rewards employees based on the organization's values. But very few organizations probe deep enough to challenge employees to introspectively discover their own values.

{ *When personal values and organizational values align . . . exponential value is realized.* }

It is more challenging than it would appear to be on the surface. In leadership workshops all over the world, I have seen the stunning realization people face when they are given a blank sheet of paper and challenged to write down their own core values.

What I have also seen, among very busy people, is once they begin to think about it—once their inner flame is stoked—they have a natural burning desire to reconnect to their values. They are inspired when they reconnect to their core. And it is good. Very good!

My hope is this little book will challenge you to search inside.

1. To **investigate** the value of knowing your core values.
2. To **indicate** your own core values.
3. To **integrate** your core values into the fabric of your life.

In doing so, I hope you become an orchardist who plants seeds of your core values into the culture of your organization.

{ *Most importantly, I hope you will be inspired to truly live your core values.* }

As you turn the pages of this book, my intent is to certainly challenge you, but my greater desire is to walk with you through the orchard of your mind, heart and soul on a journey back to your core. I am convinced when we arrive there, you will be exponentially more valuable.

I hope you can simultaneously experience this book on two different but related perspectives.

First, from a personal perspective: exploring your personal core values. In doing so, you will be more valuable to your family, your community and certainly within the organization in which you work.

Second, from an organizational perspective: thinking about the values that are the fabric of the culture in which you work. Do they exist? How well are they known? How consistently are they lived?

Most importantly, my wish as you read these pages is that you experience a sense of hope, desire and confidence. Values have a way of revealing the truth. As truth would have it … we build value through values.

And the real truth is **we can all be good to the core.** Read on!

John G Blumberg

Section One

INVESTIGATE
the Value of Values

CHAPTER 1
Applesauce ... or Not

I had never really thought about it. Apples are one of the fruits that have been used for numerous symbolisms.

Apples started, at the beginning of time, as the forbidden fruit on the Tree of Knowledge in the Garden of Eden. Ironically, it would have taken strong values—a real core discipline—to avoid them. But man failed.

Apples have been the symbol of knowledge. Ask yourself which fruit symbolizes the month of September and the start of a new school year. It's an apple for the teacher!

Apples have been an icon for good health, for an apple-a-day keeps the doctor away. And an apple also symbolizes what we cherish when we say, "You are the apple of my eye."

{ *But apples, at their very center,*
also stand as the backbone for values.
Core values. }

While growing up in the South, once in awhile I would hear someone being described as **rotten to the core.** It was the lowest of low in terms of character reference! Beyond behavior and beyond wants and needs, the essence of the accusation was that it was their foundation, the very middle, the deep inside core of that person that had spoiled. Their core values had become corrupt. In other words … they had rotted.

Even if it was true, it was more likely an evolution rather than an intentional choice. **Not many people want to intentionally rot at the core.**

Applesauce is mushy. I love the taste, but hate the consistency. **When it comes to our core, consistency is everything.** It's the core of the apple that makes the rest of the apple all that it is. The apple core is not the "good" part. **Just the most critical part.** The core stands tall and holds the very seeds of the future.

{ *The core is at the center of everything.* }

And without it, there would be no apple.

There's an insightful idea that has surfaced in the lyrics of many songs from Country to Rock. These lyrics celebrate a quote that originated in 1947 from the Chaplain of the US Senate, Peter Marshall. He simply said, **"If you don't stand for something … you will fall for anything."**

How often do we find people who don't stand for anything and therefore fall for everything? **How often do we look in the mirror and find ourselves confused on where we stand?**

CORE CHALLENGE

1 What stands tall within you?

2 Where are you currently vulnerable to falling?

"*Just as your car runs more smoothly and requires* **less energy** *to go faster and farther when the wheels are in perfect alignment,* **you perform better** *when your thoughts, feelings, emotions, goals, and values are* **in balance.** "

BRIAN TRACY

CHAPTER 2

Opening the Drawer

William Graham Sumner (1840-1912), a highly regarded Yale Professor, described reality quite well when he said, **"I have never discarded beliefs deliberately. I left them alone in a drawer. After a while I opened it and there was nothing there."** As I mentioned, I used to think it would be easy for any adult to sit and write down their core values. For ten years, I had the opportunity to co-instruct a leadership workshop in various countries around the globe. Through that experience I discovered how difficult it is for adults and students to clearly define their core values.

In the Leadership Workshop, my co-instructor taught the module that focused on core values. Consequently, it gave me a lot of time to think about what was being taught on core values and what I observed in numerous sessions. Dave Houser was my co-instructor, good friend and one

of the earliest mentors in my career. Dave did a terrific job of describing the concept of core values and then sent the participants away for what they thought would be an easy 90-minute exercise: *to write down their core values.*

Over the years, we came to know the difficult nature of this assignment. The participants would confidently begin by thinking they could write forever. Most participants were surprised at the challenge they faced in finding the right words ... or any words. Some participants wanted us to provide a list of values so they could simply check the words that seemed to apply to them. We would laugh with them as they searched for an easy out. We never did provide that list. We wanted them to open the drawer of their heart and soul and search inside. Most didn't like it. **But as they sat down and started the hard process of genuinely searching inside, eventually they seemed to love it!**

There is something of a miracle that unfolds when we reconnect to the goodness of our core. I remember when I first moved away from the city where I grew up. After a career transfer took me away from my childhood hometown, I remember going back to visit my mom. She still lived in the home in which I was raised. I slept so soundly in that little twin bed I had slept in for thousands of nights in my youth. There seemed to be little as comforting as going home to my childhood room.

I think that is what took most of these participants from discomfort and dislike to comfortably loving it:

{ *They were returning home to the goodness of the core they were born with.* }

Imagine opening the drawer of your core ...

1 Would it be dusty and look forgotten, or would it be clean, fresh and relevant?

2 What do you think you would immediately see inside?

*"Anyone can count
the seeds in an apple, but only God can*
count the number of apples
in a seed.

Robert H. Schuller

CHAPTER 3
Knowing vs. Understanding

On the surface, the concept of "core values" seems easy to comprehend. So easy that we think we understand what they are all about. The concept seems to be blindingly obvious. ***But maybe not.***

I think, for most of us, we understand the concept of core values. But that doesn't mean we understand our own core values. We have to be careful in what we assume … both individually and within the organization in which we work.

Core values are like seeds. They must be tended and cared for to meet their full potential. They flourish when they are planted in soil that is watered, fertilized and periodically weeded. I have a friend who is diligent about watering the garden of potted plants on his condo balcony. But the magic of his garden lies in his Miracle Grow® fertilizer he mixes into the water. His garden flourishes. And with a miracle mix, our personal and organizational core values can flourish as well.

Values are most alive when we have specific words to describe them, and when we remain **intentionally connected** to them. It sounds so simple, but in reality, few of us make a practice of routinely making this connection.

{ *It is the difference between cognitively knowing and genuinely understanding.* }

It is not the concept of values that is so difficult. The difficulty comes in the day-to-day world where we have to live them. We live in a world that is moving faster each day. This causes us to constantly make decisions … usually very quickly.

Ultimately, what is important is how our understanding translates into our decisions, actions and interactions. ***Our values must be lived in order for us to flourish. They are our "miracle grow."***

In the end, it is the difference of **living reactively vs. living intentionally.** The value of values begins to exponentially increase when we are living them consciously, intentionally and concretely.

Consciously
Intentionally
Concretely

Remember … be careful of what you assume you know. Knowledge is only a tool.

I have a tool box in my basement that I haven't touched in years! While tools hold enormous potential to build things and make broken things useful again … unused tools become rusty and useless. Unused, they lose their potential. Values are just like tools! They build value.

CORE CHALLENGE

1 How consciously, intentionally and concretely are you connected to your own values? Do you think you are truly living your values?

2 How consciously, intentionally and concretely are you connected to the values of the organization where you work? Do you think you are living your organization's values? Does the leadership of your organization live your organization's values?

CHAPTER 4
Under the Sea

Iwas in Honolulu to speak at a large national conference. I scheduled an extra day onto the trip since I had never been to Honolulu and because a few great friends were also at the conference.

The day after the conference, we awoke at the crack of dawn to visit Pearl Harbor. As we stood above and looked down upon the sunken USS Arizona, the depth of our experience came to life. It was moving and humbling.

Upon our return to the hotel, I had some time to spare before departing to the airport. A couple of my friends and I decided to rent a raft large enough to hold three adults. We targeted the white-capped waves, out in the distance, as our destination.

With the incoming waves, we had a hard time getting away from the shore. At first, there seemed to be enormous momentum keeping us "grounded." Slowly, but surely, we began to make progress. It seemed to get easier. We eventually got within a few feet of the whitecaps and decided to board our raft and relax as a celebration of our efforts.

It was in our moment of pause that we felt the reality of our situation. Drifting two feet out and one foot in. Again, two feet out and one foot in. We all felt the unsettling formula of our ever-so-gentle drift out to sea.

We immediately abandoned the raft and grasped for safety, with one arm holding the raft and the other arm aggressively swimming. I have never scissor-kicked so hard in my life.

Twenty minutes later we had made minimal progress.

Out of nowhere, a lifeguard on a kayak appeared on the scene asking why we were so far out. Feeling the comfort of his presence, we laughed for a moment, lightly commenting about our distance from the shore. He wasn't laughing.

"You see those big orange balls on top of the water?" the lifeguard inquired. We could see them, but they didn't look very big from where we were still struggling in the water. They did, however, give us the insight that we were basically five times farther out than we should be.

I think the lifeguard was trying to teach us a lesson. He didn't leave us, but he didn't assist us either. Forty-five minutes later we walked up on the shore. I was shaking from exhaustion. I began, for the first time, to feel the numerous cuts on my legs and feet from the sharp coral rocks lining the ocean floor.

We had briefly noticed the orange balls on our way out. We had paid little attention to them and certainly had not given any thought to their significance. **We had been too focused on our mission** to get to the white-capped waves in the distance!

The orange balls had warned us, and we unknowingly ignored them. Infrequently placed across the ocean's surface, they created an invisible line on the ocean's floor. They silently warned us not to drift beyond them regardless of our vision or mission.

{
We don't go running away from our values.
We go drifting away, and one day
wake up in a place we never meant to be,
drifting in a direction we would have never chosen.
}

CORE CHALLENGE

1 What orange balls are you missing or ignoring?

2 Who are the lifeguards in your life who can help "catch your drift?"

"*When your values are clear to you,
making decisions* **becomes easier.**"

ROY DISNEY

CHAPTER 5
More Than Orange Balls

S o what are core values anyway? Well, more than just a bunch of orange balls! But not much more. I think we try to make the concept of core values complicated, as if they are some mystical concept only the most sophisticated intellects can really understand. Not so.

In those leadership workshops, my friend Dave inspired participants with simplicity. I can still hear his voice describing values. "They are filters. They are like screens used to sift out what should be and shouldn't be. They are the rocks we stand on. They are the non-negotiables!"

Core values go beyond our behaviors and our wants. Without being intentional about our values, we live backwards. **We often let our behaviors define our values. Values should define our behaviors.**

36

Some of us let our wants become our values … *and end up needing what we want rather than wanting what we need.*

Years ago, Mike, a work colleague and dear friend, was fighting a losing battle with cancer. Through a miracle we are yet to fully comprehend, his cancer was cured. He rightfully proclaimed he had been given a second chance at life. And he didn't want to mess it up! He called to tell me he had written down some specific goals in life and wondered if I would help him be accountable to them. We lived hundreds of miles apart, so we decided we would connect once a quarter to consider how accountable he had been to his own goals. The first quarter was marginal at best. The second quarter was better. The third quarter showed marked improvement. By the last quarter of the first year of his second life, Mike was clicking on all cylinders. He found our calls to be so helpful he suggested I write down my goals and send them to him! My performance initially mirrored Mike's first quarter marginal outcome. I distinctly remember Mike relentlessly challenging me just as I had challenged him! After a few more quarterly calls he cornered me saying, "I see in your goals how much you cherish and value your young children. Yet I look at your travel schedule and there seems to be a real disconnect. Can you help me understand the gap?" I didn't need to explain it. ***My behavior had already defined it for him ... and he knew it!*** My behaviors were defining my values.

Without filters we wander aimlessly through life. We wonder why we feel empty on our life journey or in our work. We find ourselves addicted to the whims of our wants and the tasks of our work. Or we go to work each day in organizations with undefined values and wonder why the environment lacks meaningful momentum. We are simply out at sea drifting from one distraction to another.

{ *Core values create boundaries.*
Boundaries create focus, and focus minimizes drift. }

CORE CHALLENGE

1. What behaviors are currently driving the definition of your values rather than vice versa?

2. Where are you currently needing what you want rather than wanting what you need?

CHAPTER 6
Believe

One of my favorite Holiday movies is *The Polar Express,* but I fell in love with the story long before it became a popular movie. Kim, a dear friend with a huge heart, gave a copy of *The Polar Express* book to my son, Ryan, when he was five years old. It became our family's tradition to gather just before bedtime each Christmas Eve and read this beautiful story together. Kim had given us more than a book, she had given us a tradition we came to value.

We, in turn, decided to pay-it-forward. We chose one family each year who had touched our lives, and shared a new copy of *The Polar Express* book with them. When the book was made into a movie, we were excited to see the story brought to life on the cinema screen. I quickly came to love the title song of the soundtrack, *Believe.* The words of the chorus rang so true to me:

Believe in what your heart is saying, hear the melody that's playing.
There's no time to waste, there's so much to celebrate.
Believe in what you feel inside and give your dreams the wings to fly.
You have everything you need if you just BELIEVE.

– Believe, *The Polar Express*

The first and most important step of any journey is asking yourself, "Do you believe?" Once you believe, you have everything you need.

The concept of core values is no different. **You must first BELIEVE core values are valuable,** and that you can truly build value with them!

My good friend, Jim Brown, believes values are everything, and he has seen the benefits. He saw the value of values in his successful corporate career, and he has seen it in a youth football program he volunteered to coordinate for the last 30 years. Rather than a football program, it really should be called a "values program."

It all started at St. Raphael's Parish in Naperville, Illinois, with a couple hundred boys and a few teams. Today, this program serves over 2,600 youth with over 100 teams! It involves over 800 coaches and 10,000 spectators enjoy the games each Saturday. And it is all run on a commitment to the core values of the program. Jim believes everyone, the players, the coaches and the parents, benefits from the value of living the values. Jim believes one of the most critical core values guiding the program is that "all decisions are made in the best interests of the children." Living this value makes the football experience a vehicle for the total development of the child, and often for the coaches and parents as well.

I know it sounds nice. But it is not easy, especially when it might impact your season record. I remember Jim sharing with me a tough decision he had to make with the other coaches of their traveling team. A terrible rain storm left the opposing team's field in a very unsafe condition for play. Rain was forecasted to continue throughout the day. Jim knew they had a decision to make, knowing the field would be unsafe for the boys on his team. Since the other team insisted the game be played, he also knew it meant forfeiting the game should he and his coaches decide not to play. It was a tough call, but the decision was clear. When a central value of your program tells you to do what is in the best interests of the children, decisions don't become easy ... but they do become clear.

{ *Living your values can cost you; not living them can destroy you.* }

Jim is far more interested in planting seeds of character than creating the next generation of Pro Bowlers for the NFL. He is certainly interested in planting those seeds in young players. But he is just as interested in helping men, who are drawn to be coaches, demonstrate character in every aspect of their role. Jim knows the players are watching the coaches, and he deeply cares about what these players see and what they experience from these role models. He also knows that these coaches go back to work on Monday morning, and he hopes the character they practice on the sidelines during the weekend will continue throughout their business deals in the middle of the week.

Everyone in the program is required to attend a presentation on the values of the program. That includes the parents!

In an era where parents can't seem to control themselves, Jim has huge expectations for their role on the sidelines. I remember when Jim was coaching a game in which my son, Ryan, was playing. One of our parents yelled inappropriate words to a referee. Jim left the sidelines and came running over to where the parents were standing. He looked directly at the parent who had violated the values of the program and promptly asked him to leave the field. Jim is one of the kindest and gentlest men you would ever want to meet … but not in that moment. I have never seen Jim so angry.

{ *Jim believes that values are everything.* }

> *Jim doesn't believe in winning at all costs,*
> *but he does believe values have everything*
> *to do with winning.*

He should know. St. Raphael's has a long tradition of winning. So much so that others think they must somehow be cheating! Jim does know they are doing what others aren't doing … but it isn't cheating. It is simply defining, believing, living and holding everyone relentlessly accountable to a core set of values.

Companies have found the magic in values as well. I am sure, at some point, you have heard the heroic example of Tylenol®. An individual in the Chicago area decided to tamper with the contents of a number of bottles of the Tylenol® product, resulting in the death of several people and creating a public crisis. No one, including the executives at Tylenol®, knew the source or extent of the problem. What they did know was they had a set of values they believed in. And in the moment of this crisis, those values required them to literally risk the future of the entire company by pulling every bottle, in every store, in the entire nation, from store shelves. The cost of the decision was overwhelming, but through the lens of their values, the cost of not making such a drastic move was far greater. In the end, they gained enormous value from their decision. Their actions led to a revolution in the safety packaging of products in America and around the world. More importantly, during an incident where they could have easily lost the trust of the public, they not only retained trust, but exponentially increased it.

Tylenol® believed in their values and they were willing to risk everything to live them. *Each time you have a problem, it's an opportunity to demonstrate to a customer or an employee that you must act from your values ... even when times are tough.*

When it comes to being good to the core **you have everything you need if you believe!**

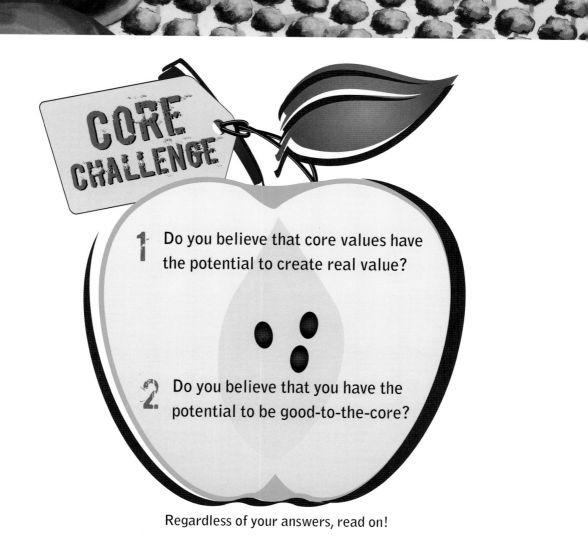

CORE CHALLENGE

1 Do you believe that core values have the potential to create real value?

2 Do you believe that you have the potential to be good-to-the-core?

Regardless of your answers, read on!

INDICATE
Your Own
Core Values

Section Two

CHAPTER 7
Pausing to Pick

Astroll through an apple orchard makes for a wonderful afternoon, but it doesn't transform a life, and certainly not an organization.

In the Midwest, visiting an apple orchard is a popular autumn tradition. But people don't just go to visit. They go to PICK! And pick they do. Not just any apple … but the ones they think will be the very best!

As a child growing up in the South, I didn't have to go to the apple orchard. We had our own apple tree in the backyard. It was huge, or at least seemed to be through the eyes of a child! The blossoms in the spring were incredible. And watching the beautiful buds produce tiny apples was a miracle in my mind. But then we had to wait and wait for the very best part: the picking!

Understanding the concept of values isn't enough. Strolling through the orchard of your mind, heart and soul isn't enough.

{ *Eventually you have to stop and pick.* }

As my parents walked out into the backyard and saw me staring at our apple tree, they would often yell out, "Wait! You have to wait until they ripen before you pick them." I, too, am now saying "WAIT!" but with a different twist. Wait to read the rest of this book! And while you wait … PICK. Start to pick your values. Don't worry about the perfect final list, just get started.

When you eat an apple you don't get to the core on the first bite. (Unless you have a really big bite!) No, it is more likely with each small bite you get just a bit closer to the core.

So pause to take a few bites. It will be helpful for you to begin your list of personal core values as we stroll forward.

The following Core Challenge exercise is just the beginning of the process. Don't let it overwhelm you. If you get stuck, put it aside for a while and come back to it. It can be helpful to let this exercise blanket a week of your life. **Notice throughout the week relationships that cross your path, decisions you have to make, challenges you have to face, empty tasks that drain you, and opportunities that fill you up!** Watch others. Reflect on disappointments and surprises that come up in the regular course of the week.

{ *Each can nurture your thinking about what you really value.* }

Each can provide insight as you continue building your list of personal core values.

1 What words come to mind as you brainstorm your potential list of core values?

2. As you think about your most valuable relationships and the really important things you do, what are the words that describe why they are important to you?

CHAPTER 8
The Formula of Why

So you started your list. Brainstorming the list can be challenging enough. Prioritizing and fine-tuning the list can be even more of a challenge. Many people frequently wonder, *"How do you know if something is simply a behavior, an emotional want, a need or truly a core value?"* It can be difficult to discern. Partially because the answer, in the end, won't be the same for everyone. What defines a core value for one person, may very well be only a want or need for another person.

While there is no black-and-white formula, the "formula of why" can help bring some personal clarification.

Look at your initial list. Take any word you consider to be a personal core value and ask yourself, "*Why* is this really important to me?" The answer to the question takes you one step closer to your real core value. Then take that answer and repeat the process, asking why that previous answer is important to you. This additional answer takes you another step closer to your real core value. You should repeat this process until the answer to the "why" question is "just because" or "it just is." At that point, you have likely reached the very core and arrived at the description of one of your core values.

"Why" is often given a bad rap as being a judgmental question. In asking "why" of others it certainly can be. **But asking "why" of ourselves as we look into the mirror of our own core values, can prove to be a powerful question that penetrates to our very core, thus revealing our truth!**

CORE CHALLENGE

1 Test the theory of "why" by choosing an idea you have written on your initial list of personal values. Go through the step of asking why it is important, and continue the process until there is simply no answer other than, "It just is!" It is with that last bite you have bitten into your core!

2 Make an initial segmentation of your list. Divide the ideas listed into what you think are behaviors vs. wants vs. needs vs. core values. There is no clear black-and-white answer. It is simply an evolution towards a clearer understanding of your core.

"Values are not just words, values are what we live by. They're about the **causes** **that we champion** *and the* **people** **we fight for.** *"*

SENATOR JOHN KERRY

CHAPTER 9

Getting From Me to We

Talking about personal values sounds … well, ***so personal.*** They certainly are personal, but I would suggest, in the end, the real benefit of our personal values extends to the families in which we live and the organizations in which we work.

I can always feel the confusion in an audience when they begin to wonder why we are talking about personal values in a corporate meeting. The answer is simple. Personal values have everything to do with business success.

{ *Personal values are the values of the business.*
Companies are made up of people.
Nothing more, nothing less. }

So often, the problem in organizations that try to create a set of values lies in how they try to create them.

The leadership of many organizations have gone away on expensive retreats to draft the core values of the business. Many come back with what are ultimately "sound bites."

These sound bites become "flavors of the month" because no one takes personal ownership of them. Shear momentum will carry the sound bites for a month or two, but in the end they are not grounded within the personal values of each member of the organization.

Unfortunately, sound bites have no bite.

For some organizations, the stated values are far too complex for any human to memorize or even vaguely remember. They are works of poetry rather than solid rocks on which to take a stand!

Other organizations seem to want to keep their values a secret. You never see them or hear about them. Others announce the core values to everyone, then move on to the next task at hand assuming everyone will just absorb this list of words and live them. It is dangerous to assume that everyone will somehow remember values, much less embrace them.

This assumption is more common than you think. Just ask sharp professionals to list the stated values of their organization. You will find most can't do it. I have asked some of the most wonderful, dedicated professionals I know to list their company's values. Most can't do it.

Very few actually read them and even fewer will absorb them, live them and hold others accountable to them. Why? ***Without their own personal core values intentionally in place, there is no sticking power.*** Think of personal values and organizational values like Velcro®. There are two sides to Velcro®. And one without the other provides no benefit! **Organizational values, without personal values, are simply blowing in the breeze.** There is no sticking power. It takes a community of workers knowing their own personal values to put teeth into the values of an organization. They are systemically connected.

Knowing our personal core values stimulates a process that can bring enormous value to an organization. The better we know our own values (and understand the value of values), the more likely we are to become interested in the values of our colleagues. Not to judge them, but to understand them. It is then, and likely only then, that an organization has any chance of its employees learning, absorbing, living and holding others accountable to their organizational values.

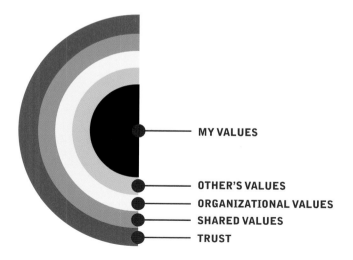

MY VALUES

OTHER'S VALUES

ORGANIZATIONAL VALUES

SHARED VALUES

TRUST

For many of us, the problem is that we work on *being interesting instead of interested.* And it's usually because our motives are not grounded in a strong set of personal core values. Tim Sanders, one of my favorite writers, asks this critical question when it comes to relationships:

{ *"Are you going to be interesting or interested?"* }

In organizations, when we know our own core, we are much more likely to want to know the core of someone else. And when we know the core of someone else, we are much more likely to function more effectively together. We truly become a community that knows each other, cares about each other and desires to be successful … *together.*

Values don't just happen. It takes time. It takes dialogue. It takes commitment. It will cost you, but it is a wise investment. It is good business. It is in this intersection of the core that real benefits begin to sprout. Trust and respect begin to soar. Retention increases. And service becomes genuine.

It all starts with individuals knowing their own core values. It is then and only then, that an organization has any chance of its employees knowing and caring about the organization's core values.

I can count on two hands the number of organizations where I have asked an employee to tell me their organization's values and he or she was actually able to tell me. Some know a list of values exists and with time can search and eventually find them. Others have no idea if a list of values exists, and sadly enough, there are many more organizations than I would like to imagine that simply don't operate on a set of intentional values. More often than not, they operate on a budgeted set of financials for the next quarter, month or week. And we wonder why we continue to have fallout on Wall Street and Main Street.

{ *Bailouts don't prevent future fallouts. Values do.* }

Just because you don't have a list of values doesn't mean you don't operate on a set of values. But without the list, it is not likely to be the set on which you really want to operate! And we wonder why we witness failure after failure in our business community. I have often heard that making no decision is a decision. The same holds true for values.

{ *Operating without a set of values . . . is a value!* }

Before it sounds like I am organization bashing, let's be certain that the responsibility goes both directions. Often, employees sit in judgment as to whether their company is operating on a set of values, instead of looking into the mirror and asking themselves how they can **take ownership for being a role model of corporate values.**

Imagine this. You have taken the time to create your list of personal values. You are then handed a list of your organization's values. **Once you have walked through the orchard of your own heart, mind and soul to discover, fine-tune and absorb your own personal core values, I suspect you will see your organization's values in a whole new light ... test me on this.**

If your employer has a list of corporate values, go grab the list (even if you have to do an intranet search for them!). Slowly go down the list and think about each value listed. **Chances are you will see them in a whole different light when they are filtered through the lenses of your own core values.** I trust you will see *and feel* a difference. You will likely begin to feel a personal emotional attachment to the organizational values.

Hopefully you will see each and every value as a genuine opportunity to bring a piece of yourself to the organization. It is at this point these corporate values become easier to learn, absorb, and live. Ultimately, it becomes easier to hold yourself and your coworkers accountable.

It is here that even "sound bites" have the potential to become values with teeth! **And it is here you can begin to build value with values!**

CORE CHALLENGE

1 Grab a list of the stated core values of your current organization. If you aren't aware of this list, do some research to see if one exists on the organization's intranet or by "asking around." If one simply doesn't exist, think of how you can begin to get the attention of the right executives to create one (even if you have to start by making a list of values for your group, department or division).

2 Take your personal list of values and your organization's list of values and put them side-by-side. Go down the list of organizational values, using your own personal values as a resource, to see how you can take personal responsibility for bringing the organizational values to life. Hopefully you will begin to see the organizational list of values as a real opportunity to find meaning and fulfillment in your work, as well as a means to bring greater value to your role.

*"On a group of theories
one can found a school;
but on a group of values
one can found a culture,
a civilization, a new way of
living together among men."*

IGNAZIO SILONE

CHAPTER 10

Finding Values in Heroic Proportions

I n my keynotes on leadership, I will often begin the presentation on the following premise:

> { *It is going to be about what you do,*
> *but first about who you are.* }

Values are about who you are. They are brought to life by what you do. This is why we can often find great examples of meaningful values through noticing the heroes in our life.

It can be very difficult to start by listing your values on a blank sheet of paper. While it was important to brainstorm that initial list, it is helpful to populate the options from other angles.

Sometimes we can come in through the back door. A good place to start is by making a list of the *people you hold in highest esteem.* Heroes and role models. People who have inspired you. Then think about the verbs, the nouns, the adjectives and the adverbs that paint a picture of who they are. Write down as many of these descriptive words as you can.

If these people are heroic in your mind's eye, then often some of their description is a reflection of your own inner core.

> "*Our values are not luxuries,* **but necessities.**
> *They are not the salt in our bread,*
> *but* **the bread itself.**"
>
> JIMMY CARTER

You can do the same for organizations you have come to admire. Make a list of words that describe your experience with them. Then think about the verbs, the nouns the adjectives and the adverbs that paint a picture of the culture of those organizations. Write down as many descriptive words as you can.

These two exercises should prime your pump to continue thinking about your own personal values and pondering a set of values that would create an inspiring work environment.

And I hope it will inspire you
to take ownership for the values in
{ *your own organization, whether that means* }
cultivating a great set of already stated values,
or becoming the influence to
create them from scratch.

CORE CHALLENGE

1 Make a list of your heroes and words that describe them. Peruse the list looking for words that are examples of your own values. Add them to your values list for consideration.

2 Take a moment to write a thank-you note to one of the heroes or role models you have listed. It is guaranteed to touch the life of whomever you send it to, and it is guaranteed to inspire you to be heroic for others through your own set of core values.

CHAPTER 11
Strolling Through the Orchard

In the leadership workshop we taught—from Australia to France, from London to Prague, and throughout the United States—we never provided a canned list of values to participants so they could simply check those applicable to them. In retrospect, I think we should have provided that list. Not to dumb it down, make it any easier, or stifle their imagination, but simply to stimulate thinking.

Most people will conceptually conclude that values are important. And it is precisely at this point the process stalls. In the spirit of simply stimulating your thinking, I thought we would take a walk through the orchard. Look around as you stroll through the orchard of the following pages. *Let your mind, heart and soul wonder as you wander.* Check out the apples hanging on these next few pages. Some will be a perfect match for you. You would never pick all the apples in the orchard. Likewise with these pages, pick whatever might be useful. Some may not be so apparent on the surface. That's ok. Split those open. Look inside. **They may contain seeds of the incredible potential that waits to grow within you.**

This is a well kept orchard! It is organized into four rows. As you stroll, I hope you will come one step closer to your CORE:

Row 1	Row 2	Row 3	Row 4
Center	**Own**	**Renew**	**Engage**

Take a stroll for yourself. Beyond values, you might just rediscover something else. Like your passion and meaningful success. Let's stroll.

Row 1

Center
yourself

Even the "core" has a center. And the center is the backbone of the core. Without it there is ultimately no core. I have often said there is a question that tests the validity of the things on your "personal core values" list. It is this: would you be willing to lose everything to stay true to this value? It is a difficult question. Is it a requirement of every single word on your core list? Maybe not every word ... but certainly every value you place in the center!

{ HONESTY AND INTEGRITY }

Many often think of honesty and integrity as two sides of the same coin. They may very well be two fruits of the same tree, but there is an interesting variation between them. I have come to see this through the work of leadership guru Warren Bennis, when he made a useful distinction between the two. He describes honesty as simply *telling the truth.* When someone asks you a question, you tell them the truth. All meaningful relationships depend on honesty: at home, at work, and in our community. If there ever was a critical center to the core, it is honesty.

Jim LaBorde was a great mentor to me in my professional career and life. He was helpful in many ways, because he would always tell me the truth. I remember a plaque he had in his office that said, **"Now that I've told you the truth am I your enemy?"** Honesty is not only about telling the truth, it is also about absorbing the truth from others.

Warren Bennis describes integrity in a different way: *doing what you say you will do.* It seems to me it is a subset of honesty. I grew up in the early years of my professional career in an environment where this kind of integrity was a given. You were absolutely expected to follow through on your commitments. You simply did what you said you were going to do, and delivered it by the time you said you were going to do it.

I found a different experience after I moved into the speaking profession and had the honor of serving as President of the Illinois Chapter of the

National Speaker's Association. We had a great board of directors, but there were some gaps. Especially when a board member would commit to take action on an item, only to show up at our next board meeting without a trace of recollection of that commitment. When we don't follow through on our commitments, we lack integrity. I know there are times where I have lacked integrity. Technology, speed and mounting volumes of expectations make integrity even more challenging. Integrity requires focus, discipline and being intentional about your commitments.

The bottom-line of integrity is doing what you say you will do. How honest are you about that?

{ PURE MOTIVES }

Our motives beg the question … WHY! Why are you doing what you are doing? What is your *motivation?* When you are intentional about your values, your motives are more likely to be pure. *Keeping your motives pure can be a value in itself.*

Continuing to do a safety-net check on your motives can be healthy. It is easy to begin a project, a career or a life-time passion with the best of intentions. It is often said that power or success corrupts. We don't have to look much beyond our own backyard to see corruption in business, politics and churches. And more often than not, where you see corruption, you will find motives gone astray. I say "gone astray" because the likelihood is that these wayward motives originally started with pure intentions.

Speed, experience, confidence, power, success, and failure, can all gradually move our motives to a place where we would never want them to be.

{ ON-PURPOSE }

Closely tied to motives, yet different, is a sense of being on-purpose. No society on earth has ever been exposed to so many choices … or distractions. It is no wonder how we can so easily wander from our real purpose, whether it is wandering from our personal focus or an organizational focus.

As an entrepreneur, I am constantly faced with attractive opportunities. Some are clear mismatches and are easy to decline. The majority, however, are much harder to discern. I have to continually come back to the basic question, *"Is this bringing me closer or further away from my sense of purpose?"* Purpose can be a critical value for keeping us centered and focused in a world moving so fast it can easily blur any vision we may have for the future.

In the early days of my speaking career, I sent out a series of promotional postcards. Each had a question on the front with an answer on the back. The first set of promotional cards was designed for those hiring speakers on college campuses. The question on the first postcard in this series read, *"What is better than sleeping-in?"* I figured most college students would have a one-word answer: NOTHING! The answer on the back begged a more thoughtful insight. Better than sleeping in is *waking up on-purpose.*

In 2002, Rick Warren released his book *Purpose Driven Life.* It would prove to be a run-away smash-hit selling millions of copies in the first four years! I am sure there are a lot of reasons why that book went sky-high, but none more likely than we are simply desperate for a sense of purpose. It is hard to find meaningful purpose without truly understanding our own core values. It might serve us well to have being on-purpose as one of our centering core values!

{ RESPECT }

We can talk a great game of respect. Living it can be a different story. It all depends on *how deep the value of respect runs within you.* It is easy to respect those who are like you or think the same way you do. It can be more challenging to respect someone who is very different from us or sees the world differently than we do.

The depth of our value for respect may very well change what we see in others. Instead of looking for what is different, we may find it easier to focus on what we have in common. Or it may allow us to focus on what is good in others. A friend of mine always says the four most important letters in the English alphabet, when consecutively lined-up together, are I-C-N-U. In other words, what is it that *I see in you?*

One organization I have come to love and admire is Best Buddies International. Best Buddies works with high school and college-aged individuals, as well as adults, who have intellectual disabilities such as Down Syndrome. I have learned many things from those who dedicate their lives to individuals with intellectual disabilities and from those with intellectual disabilities. One thing they have taught me comes from a Central African customary greeting they have adopted. Simply put, this greeting is **I SEE YOU!** It is a brilliant recognition of the individual. The standard American greeting "How Are You?" is often said without regard to a true answer. Saying "I See You" means *you recognize another as a person, as an equal, as a fellow human being, and as a friend.*

Best Buddies recently asked me to speak at its National Leadership Conference. It was an honor to speak to over a thousand high school and college students. Yet the highlight was when they asked me, as a professional speaker, to work with about 25 participants with intellectual disabilities as they prepared to give a presentation on the closing day of the conference. I have never felt such unconditional love and respect. When I arrived they were complete strangers. When I departed they were best buddies. They helped me understand what it means when they say, "I See You!"

What we can see in others may very well be brought into focus in direct correlation to how deep the need for respect runs in the center of our own core.

{ BELIEF IN SELF }

While "respect" opens us up to believe in others, another part of our core could very well be to believe in ourselves. In fact, it may be the very value that teaches us to believe in others and to help them to believe in themselves.

When we believe in ourselves from the very center of who we are, *it changes everything.* Maybe more than anything, it changes our need to prove ourselves to others. It more likely allows us to let our actions speak for themselves.

You have probably met those people who are always trying to prove how great they are (usually telling you about it!). More often than not, they are not actually trying to convince you of their worth. They are trying to convince themselves. ***When we believe in ourselves from within, we can put less energy in trying to get approval from others,*** and can better use that energy for building authentic relationships.

{ HUMILITY }

Belief in self can be an empowering core value as long as it doesn't move one to pride and arrogance. *Humility is like the grounding wire.* It is the very value that can bring all your other values to life in a meaningful way. Humility helps us remember our life journey is not about us. Earlier I mentioned Jim Brown's football program at St. Raphael. Jim teaches his players a powerful lesson about the benefits of humility. He says, "When you are saying, 'hey look at me!' no one else is usually saying, 'hey look at you!'" It is a simple but powerful lesson about humility. *If you want to get noticed, be humble.*

HUMILITY CONTINUOUSLY PURIFIES
ALL THE OTHER VALUES THAT HAVE THE
POTENTIAL TO CENTER US:
HONESTY, INTEGRITY, PURE MOTIVES, RESPECT,
AND BELIEF IN OURSELVES.

So, what seeds sit at the very center of your core?

Row 2

Own
your work

Ownership is a key ingredient of finding fulfillment in our work and in our lives. When we don't create an attitude of ownership, we leave ourselves open to the whims and ways of circumstance and the choices of others. Ownership is going beyond pulling your own weight, and beyond doing your share. It resides in a place of doing what needs to be done. Regardless.

{ RESPONSIBLE AND ACCOUNTABLE }

At the very core of owning your work is the willingness to be responsible for and held accountable for all you do.

Many like to play the blame game. They are like a mirror in a light show, deflecting the light (the blame) in a different direction rather than simply absorbing it.

84

Others like to play the victim. The problem with declaring yourself the victim is you give up control to someone else. Being responsible and accountable takes us to a new level that helps build the margin we need in order to absorb the blows of blame when they come our direction.

While being responsible and accountable helps us absorb the blame aimed in our direction, it more importantly inspires us to use the gifts within us to the greatest extent possible. ***Take the responsibility to be accountable!***

{ QUALITY }

This begs the question ... responsible and accountable to what level? We live in an urgent and immediate kind of world. And the quality of our work and responsiveness can suffer in the midst of the speed. It can be tempting to deliver short of our very best. And when it happens we know it, there is something inside us that wilts just a bit.

Valuing quality has the ability to inspire us beyond the day-to-day challenges, and insurmountable obstacles. ***Consistently having a desire to own*** *our work through quality* allows us to increase the value we bring to any of our work.

{ CREATIVITY }

Owning our work goes beyond recreating what we have known with excellence. It is daring to create something totally new. The yet to be known. The yet to be seen. The not yet tested. We are all creative. I learned this from Kathy Kolbe and all of her work in understanding our natural instincts. Many people don't think they are creative, but, in the end, that is just a cop-out. Kathy Kolbe would tell us we are all creative … we just create in different ways. *The question isn't whether you are creative or not.* It is a question of whether you value your creativity.

{ COMMITMENT AND PERSISTENCE }

Staying power is a powerful thing. And the more daring you are, the more critical it becomes. Most people can start. Far fewer can finish. Most people will give up on process, procedures, risks, adventures, techniques or initiatives because they don't give it enough time. Hence, the flavor-of-the-month syndrome in many organizations … just going from one new initiative to another. ***They quit on it too soon.*** And in the end, they quit on themselves and on those around them.

There will always be barriers. The key becomes our effectiveness at staying with something, not only through the barriers, but through the mundane day-to-day actions that move toward greatness.

It is important we celebrate interim success. Values are much more about the journey rather than the destination. Each success along the way needs to be celebrated. Each value sustained in the midst of setbacks and challenges needs to be celebrated. These tiny celebrations will nourish your commitment and persistence.

Commitment and persistence are grounded in how much you value owning your work.

DO YOU OWN YOUR WORK OR DOES YOUR WORK OWN YOU?

Row 3

Renew
your spirit

Simply put, you cannot give what you do not have.
And you cannot have what you do not replenish.
Our spirit is like a bucket with a leak. It is drained by
all the activities of our everyday life. It leaks over time
and eventually is emptied unless we have a process to
refill it.

{ ADVENTURE }

Life is truly an adventure. If for no other reason than that the future ultimately is a mystery. Much of life is a mystery. But we try to drain the adventure of all its mystery. We try to dumb-it-down into routines, schedules and self-created (or forced upon us) expectations of exactly how life should be lived.

88

While technology has, in itself, been an adventure, I am beginning to wonder if it has created a whole new level of demands that takes us to such a reactive stage in life that there is no time to dream. No time to let life be truly an adventure in our work, in our family and in our community.

The very challenges that disturb us are, in the end, seeds for new adventure. However, without valuing adventure, we most likely declare ourselves victims of the bumps in the road.

Developing a thirst for adventure can change how we see everything. And while adventure can be draining, it can also *renew your spirit.*

{ LAUGHTER }

Those who take themselves too seriously tend to live a much rougher life. If there is one thing most people are starving from, it is from lack of laughter. The ability to laugh has everything to do with the quality of relationships … with others and with ourselves. I get much more done with the people I tend to laugh with. *We work better together, we listen to each other more, and we have a more genuine respect for each other.*

Laughter is not a joke. It is serious business. It renews our spirit and refreshes our soul. Can you remember the last time you had a gut wrenching laugh? After such an episode I have so often heard people say, "Oh, I really needed that!" And needing it is an understatement!

{ OPTIMISM }

How we see things is simply a choice. The circumstances in which we find ourselves may be beyond our control, but the *response* we choose is not! And how we respond has everything to do with how we have come to see all that is around us.

Some think that either you are an optimistic person or not. Martin Seligman, Ph.D. begs to differ in his book *Learned Optimism.* He sees optimism as a choice.

I often recall the famous quote from Charles Dickens' book *A Tale of Two Cities*:

> *"It was the best of times, it was the worst of times, it was the age of wisdom, it was the age of foolishness, it was the epoch of belief, it was the epoch of incredulity, it was the season of light, it was the season of darkness, it was the spring of hope, it was the winter of despair, we had everything before us, we had nothing before us."*

I always like to take this excerpt and suggest it is a great opportunity for choice. Are you going to have the best of times or the worst? Live in a spring of hope or a winter of despair? Are you living in a season of light or a time of darkness? For most every situation where you find a person who has been defeated by a set of circumstances, you will find a hero who has triumphantly risen from the ashes of a similar set of circumstances. Most often the difference is choice. And choice is actionable!

When optimism is an integral part of renewing our spirit, we are most likely to follow the way of the Phoenix and rise from the ashes.

{ CURIOSITY }

Our ability to change is one thing. Our sense of curiosity is another. I think one of the great joys in life is watching a baby in one of his or her moments of discovery. They have an innocent curiosity about everything. Most of us lose that sense of curiosity in the busyness of life or when we think we've got it all figured out. When we lose our sense of curiosity we are most likely to disengage. We may robotically continue through life, but are more often than not just going through the motions.

We live in an incredible world. *There is so much to discover in our work, our relationships, and yes, our challenges.*

BUT WE MUST FIRST REOPEN OUR EYES TO THE WONDER OF IT ALL AND IN DOING SO REENGAGE OUR CURIOSITY.

"Happiness *is that state of consciousness which proceeds from the* **achievement of one's values."**

AYN RAND

Row 4

Engage
your potential

The greatest recession in an economy shouldn't be measured by financial models … but rather by models of engagement. Marcus Buckingham and the Gallup organization have documented amazingly low levels of genuine employee engagement. Engagement can certainly be encouraged by organizational efforts, but ultimately it is driven by one's own personal values.

{ STEWARDSHIP }

Early in my professional career, I engrained in my whole being the importance of stewardship … leaving something behind better than it was left for you.

Entitlement is the arch-enemy of stewardship. Entitlement is an illusion about what is due to us. Stewardship is the reality of our due to others as a response to what has been given to us.

Stewardship says there is something better to be left behind. Not devoured, but improved upon and left as your gift for others. It rests in the spirit of "paying it forward" for what others have done for you.

As a value, it changes the context of everything. It is your insurance policy against selling out the long-term for your short-term gain.

{ SERVICE }

We talk a good game of service. Many organizations have invested heavily in customer-service training programs. Most of these programs teach skills and often reduce service down to a mechanical process. And what we get is a process for "servicizing." It is simply going through the motions. ***Unfortunately, in a country that prides itself on a service-driven economy, service has never been worse!***

There is nothing mechanical about service. Service is about making a connection. Genuine service is impossible to achieve without fully engaging in our work, and more importantly, fully engaging in the moment with individual people. Not with a process or a procedure, but with a person.

And I am convinced, when we lack a spirit of service, the customer is not the ultimate loser. We are. We rob ourselves of the greatest opportunity offered by our work. *It is no wonder so many people find their work to be a chore rather than a great opportunity to serve.*

{ ATTITUDE }

I recently did a feature article in my monthly e-newsletter, which is titled *The Front Porch.* The article focused on one simple thought: *attitude.* As in checking our attitude! There has only been one other article that has gotten more response than this one. It seems it hit a chord with a lot of people who had let their attitude slip away. And *when our attitude slips away our engagement fades away.*

I have found, more often than not, when I simply do an attitude check I find it significantly easier to reengage. If we want to stay engaged, valuing our attitude can be really important to our core.

{ FORGIVENESS }

Yes, forgiveness. It is a value that might surprise you. It certainly surprised me.

It was one of those moments you remember exactly where you were when you heard the news. Kind of like where you were the moment you heard of the assassination of John F. Kennedy or Martin Luther King. Or where you were the moment you heard of the space shuttle explosion—both of them. Or where you were and who you were with on Tuesday morning, September 11, 2001.

I recall another event. I was on my way to do a book signing at a Barnes & Noble back in my hometown of Memphis. I was just getting ready to exit I-40 and was listening to the radio. It was the "top-of-the-hour" so the national news update was airing. This time it wasn't the national news event itself that created a permanent memory of where I was, it was what happened after the event. The national reporter was interviewing a resident of the Amish community who, just a couple of days earlier, had suffered the unthinkable. A man walked into a school murdering five precious children from their community and then killed himself. The reporter asked a number of questions and then asked what seemed to be a fairly general question, "Where do you go from here?" The Amish woman being interviewed didn't even hesitate as she replied *"straight to forgiveness."* I wish I could have seen the expression on the face of the radio reporter, although her stunned response of "excuse me?" was all I really needed to hear. It was immediately clear that the interviewee was confident and clear while the reporter was totally confused. It was as if the concept of forgiveness, especially in these set of circumstances, couldn't begin to penetrate the psyche of the reporter. And if I hadn't found her response so stunning myself, I probably wouldn't have remembered where I was at that moment. I remember exactly.

But beyond stunned, it got me seriously thinking about *the value of forgiveness in life and in business.* I have seen the values statements of numerous organizations. But I have never seen one of them— ever—list anything close to the word forgiveness. Maybe because none of them lists anything close to the word humility, either. Most of the values statements list much stronger and bolder proclamations like quality, innovation and excellence. But what could be more excellent in the culture of any organization than a fabric of forgiveness? It may, in fact, change everything.

Imagine being measured with monthly metrics on how effectively you forgive and move-on. Before you write this off as soft and inappropriate for shop talk, begin to ponder the bottom-line impact of grudges, politics and silos in the workplace. Or begin to imagine the cost of gossip perpetuated by a longing for revenge.

Then *imagine what the culture of an organization might look like if forgiveness was woven into the fabric* of that environment. Think of the impact on relationships, on collaboration, on retention and eventually on the bottom-line. *Then finally imagine what forgiveness might look like on the list of your own personal core values.*

IF THERE IS ANYTHING THAT MIGHT BE CONSIDERED A CRITICAL INGREDIENT OF ENGAGING YOURSELF, IT CERTAINLY SEEMS LIKE FORGIVENESS IS IT!

Section Three

INTEGRATE
Your Values
and Actions

CHAPTER 12
One Step at a Time

It all sounds so easy. So simple. Then why is it so hard? If it were easy, more people would be able to immediately articulate their core values and would excel at living them every day.

How many people have you met who have said they wouldn't want to operate from their values?

How many corporate leaders have you met who would admit to being comfortable operating without some level of values as the rudder for their organizations?

The problem isn't the theory. The problem isn't our desire. The problem is actually living it every hour of every day in a world of shortcuts, short-term thinking and distractions.

> *Values become easier when we*
> *truly believe core values really do have value,*
> *and that they create value.*

While this is a short section of this book, it is likely the most challenging of all.

It is the process of integrating your personal core values into your daily life. One thing for certain, most everything will challenge you on this: circumstances, time, relationships, those who are reactively living their life for short-term gain, and of course, the voices in your head that may say, "Just give it up … it is too difficult … too costly!"

This process is about one step at a time. Sometimes that will be a step forward and sometimes a step backwards. Sometimes it will be about stepping in place with a sense of patience. And sometimes it will be about stepping out to help others. Sometimes it will be about not stepping at all while you simply anchor yourself to get back up. But with enough practice, you will go from stepping to dancing through your life. It will simply begin to flow. For an individual, it will become a way of life. For an organization, it will become the fabric of its culture. But once internalized, for both, it will enhance its intrinsic value.

Every walk through an orchard starts with the first step. Being able to see the path ahead can help make the journey a bit more efficient. So let's take a moment to look back over our shoulders to where we have been, and to see where the path might lead:

1 **Make a list** of your personal core values. Start with a personal brainstorming session. Don't feel like you have to do it all in one sitting. Set a timeframe of a week or a month and carry the list with you wherever you go. As various possibilities cross your mind, add them to the list. Don't feel like you have to filter your ideas. This is simply your personal research into your own mind, heart and soul. *Just let the ideas flow!*

2 Once you are satisfied you have a fairly complete list of possibilities, **start the process of segmenting** the list into what you believe to

be your behaviors, your wants, your needs and then ultimately, your core values. Don't forget to use the formula of "why" to help you distinguish between the variations of these categories.

3   **Finalize what you believe** to be your list of core values. You will likely continue, for some time, to "fine-tune" this list, but it should represent a fairly solid picture of your core.

4   **Investigate the values** of your own organization. If they exist, make the effort to thoroughly understand them.

5   **Compare your list** of personal core values to these organizational values. Look for opportunities to engage your values around these organizational values. Look for possible disconnects and bring a sense of reconciliation around these differences.

6   If your organization does not have a list of organizational values, investigate why. In a way that builds upon your own values, **consider reaching out** to volunteer your services to create an initiative that will define these organizational values. Look for gaps in current opera-

tions, performance and relationships that are being undermined because of undefined values.

7   **Work relentlessly** to start intentionally living your values every day … even when it costs you. These costs are simply investments in a greater value.

8   **Find ways to replenish** your desire to live your core values. Remember, you cannot give what you do not have, and you cannot have what you do not replenish! *Celebrate the smallest of successes.*

9   **Encourage others** to follow your example. Work with them on their own struggle to define their personal values.

10 **Hold your organization accountable** to the values it espouses. In doing so you will create an equity that goes beyond the balance sheet.

"*The individual increasingly comes to* **know who he is** *through the stand he takes when he expresses his ideas, values, beliefs, and convictions and through the* **declaration and ownership** *of his feelings.*"

CLARK MOUSTAKAS

1

CHAPTER 13
One Final Thought

With all that has been said, I think you have to ask yourself a final question. **Why bother with this at all?** It is an important question. Most people I know who are trying to genuinely understand their own core values, and who patiently, yet persistently, try to live them, have come to a place of understanding that life is bigger than self.

Maybe it goes back to humility. But I think it's bigger than that. *It is bigger than any organization, any family and any community.* And in this realization they find something within themselves that inspires them to not only start this walk in the orchard, but to finish it.

You need to answer this too. You don't have to start here, but ultimately you have to end here. Because you will need this answer along the journey of trying to live your core values.

Developing your core values does not promise you a smooth ride. In fact, on the surface, it will likely cause you to hit a few bumps or potholes along the way.

{ *As you slowly, but surely, commit to living your values, it will preserve the goodness of your core.* }

FINAL CHALLENGE

Do you believe ...
truly believe
you are good to the core?

It is where we end, but where you begin.
The truth is you are good to the core.
And when you truly believe ... you will be amazed the
value you can create with your values!

About the Author

John G. Blumberg

John speaks with corporations, professional associations and universities across America, sharing insights on developing leaders of substance and building cultures of genuine service.

As a full-time professional speaker, John has reached audiences in 10 countries on 3 continents. The National Speakers Association has recognized John with the designation of Certified Speaking Professional. The CSP is the highest earned designation in the speaking profession and is held by less than 10% of the members of the International Federation of Professional Speakers. He is a past president of the National Speakers Association's Illinois Chapter.

John started his career as a CPA at Arthur Andersen. After four years, he shifted his focus from numbers to people where he then spent another 14 years in human resources and recruiting … including worldwide recruiting responsibilities for Andersen. In 1996, John decided to leave a firm and a position he loved to follow his dream into the world of professional speaking.

John is also the author of *Silent Alarm.* It is a parable of hope for busy professionals. For some, it is a message of inspiration … and for others, a wake-up call for their very survival. For everyone … it is an experience you won't soon forget!

John lives in Naperville, Illinois, with his wife, Cindy, and their three children.

John can be reached at **www.keynoteconcepts.com**

If you have enjoyed this book we invite you to check out our entire collection of gift books, with free inspirational movies, at **www.simpletruths.com**. You'll discover it's a great way to inspire friends and family, or to thank your best customers and employees.